To my children, Kyle, Evan and Kristin — together we find the way past our fears — C.H.

For Tristan and Chas., my favorite explorers — K.F.

For Tara, who lit the path — T.F. & E.F.

Paperback edition published by Tundra Books, 2018

Tundra Books, an imprint of Penguin Random House Canada Young Readers, a Penguin Random House Company

Library and Archives Canada Cataloguing in Publication

Hadfield, Chris, 1959–, author
The darkest dark / Chris Hadfield with Kate Fillion ; illustrations by the Fan Brothers.
Originally published: Toronto, Ontario : Tundra Books, 2016.
ISBN 978-0-7352-6482-3 (softcover)
1. Hadfield, Chris, 1959– —Childhood and youth—Juvenile literature.
2. Hadfield, Chris, 1959– —Juvenile literature. 3. Astronauts—Canada—Biography—
Juvenile literature. 4. Autobiographies. I. Fillion, Kate, author II. Fan, Eric, illustrator
III. Fan, Terry, illustrator IV. Title.
TL789.85.H34A3 2018   j629.450092   C2017-908074-1

Published simultaneously in the United States of America by Little, Brown Books for Young Readers,
a division of Hachette Book Group, New York, and in the United Kingdom by Pan Macmillan, London.

Edited by Tara Walker and Farrin Jacobs
The artwork in this book was rendered in graphite and colored digitally.
Interior photo credits: p. 42, all photos courtesy of Chris Hadfield; p. 43, all photos of Chris courtesy of NASA;
photo of Chris and Albert courtesy of Terry Fan and Eric Fan.
The text was set in Garamond.
Printed and bound in China

www.penguinrandomhouse.ca

1 2 3 4 5   22 21 20 19 18

THE DARKEST DARK

Written by **CHRIS HADFIELD** and **KATE FILLION**

Illustrated by **THE FAN BROTHERS**

tundra

Chris was an astronaut. An important and very busy astronaut.

When it was time to take a bath, he told his mother,
"I'd love to, but I'm saving the planet from aliens."

When it was time to get out of the bath and go to bed,
he told his father — politely, because astronauts are always polite —
"Sorry, no can do. I'm on my way to Mars."

An astronaut's work is never done,
so astronauts do not like to sleep.

But their parents do.

"You're a big boy now," said Chris's father.
"You have to sleep in your own bed."

And Chris tried, he really did, but his room was dark. Very, very dark.

The kind of dark that attracts the worst sort of aliens.

But his parents meant it.

Chris. Was. Going. To. Sleep.
In. His. Own. Bed. *Tonight.*

His mom and dad checked under his bed and in the closet and even in his underwear drawer. They declared the room 100 percent alien-free.

They tucked Chris in. They turned on the night-light. They even gave him a special bell to ring if he was nervous.

Toronto Daily Star

Wednesday, July 16, 1969 — 64 pages

MOON-BOUND

8:32 a.m.
blastoff

"The spirit of the American people as well as the world will soar with you on your flight to the moon."

—President Nixon

Stories on Pages 4 and 5

Apollo 11 crew, enjoying their final dinner here on Earth before Wednesday morning's blast-off. Buzz Aldrin, lunar module pilot, digs into a steak.

"Spacemen Will Be Spee
At Over 24,000 mph"

They took away the bell.

And then his father said something that worried Chris even more than the dark did. "One more peep, young man, and I'm afraid we'll all be too tired to go next door tomorrow."

But tomorrow would be a special day. A very special day. Chris *had* to go next door. His life pretty much depended on it.

So Chris stayed in his own bed. Without a peep. It took a long time to fall asleep, but when he did, he had his favorite dream . . .

He flew his spaceship all the way to the Moon.

The next day seemed to last forever. But finally, when the Moon was shining over the lake and the summer wind was ruffling the leaves of the trees, Chris ran next door.

The house was already full of people, all gathered
around the TV — the only TV on the whole island.

Chris found a spot where he could see through the crowd.
And what he saw was . . .

Astronauts. Real, live astronauts. On the actual, far-away Moon.
They were wearing puffy white suits and jumping for joy —
jumping so high, because there was so much less gravity there.

The grown-ups huddled around the TV were amazed. Their whole lives long, they'd never expected to see this sight. Even Chris (who had been to the Moon just the night before) was amazed. He'd never really noticed how *dark* it was there.

Outer space was the darkest dark ever.

That night, Chris did a little experiment.
He turned off all the lights in his room,
even the night-light. It was still dark.
Very, *very* dark. There were still shadows
that looked a little, well, alien. Nothing
had changed.

But Chris had changed.

He'd seen that the darkness of the
universe was so much bigger and
deeper than the darkness in his room,
but he was not afraid. He wanted to
explore every corner of the night sky.

For the first time, Chris could see
the power and mystery and velvety
black beauty of the dark.

And, he realized, you're never really alone there.
Your dreams are always with you, just waiting.
Big dreams, about the kind of person you want to be.

Wonderful dreams about the life you will live.

Dreams that actually can come true.

ABOUT CHRIS HADFIELD

Growing up, Chris Hadfield spent every summer at his family's cottage on Stag Island in southern Ontario. Like just about everyone else on the island, the Hadfields didn't have a television set, so late in the evening of July 20, 1969, Chris and his family went to a neighbor's cottage to watch the *Apollo 11* landing on TV. When he saw Neil Armstrong step onto the surface of the Moon, Chris's life changed forever. He knew he wanted to be an astronaut too.

At the time, it was impossible. For one thing, he wasn't a grown-up yet. For another, all of NASA's astronauts were American. Canadians weren't even allowed to apply for the job.

But Chris decided to start getting ready, just in case things ever changed. He worked hard at school, learning everything he could about science, rockets and space. As a teenager, he learned how to fly gliders, and then, after graduating from military college, he became a fighter pilot. Later, he became a test pilot who helped make military aircraft safer. In 1992, almost twenty-three years after that summer night on Stag Island, Chris's dream came true: the newly formed Canadian Space Agency chose him to be an astronaut.

Since then, he has orbited the Earth thousands of times on three separate missions. Most recently, Chris was in space for nearly five months, from December 2012 to May 2013, when he served as the first Canadian Commander of the International Space Station (ISS).

Today, Chris travels the world teaching people about space, sharing the beautiful photographs he took and playing the songs he recorded on the space station. On summer nights, he likes to sit on his dock on Stag Island, watching for the ISS to pass by overhead. Even in the darkest dark, on a moonless night, the spaceship's light is clearly visible.

A MESSAGE FROM CHRIS

Being in the dark can feel scary . . . but it's also an amazing place. The dark is where we see the stars and galaxies of our universe. The dark is where we find the Northern Lights shimmering and get to wish on shooting stars. And it was quietly in the dark where I first decided who I was going to be and imagined all the things I could do. The dark is for dreams — and morning is for making them come true.

Chris Hadfield

Chris Hadfield

My first spaceship, 1964.

My family (that's me in the striped shirt), 1966.

Excited to be a glider pilot, 1975.

Getting into the rocket that will take me
to the International Space Station, 2012.

My first spacewalk
(and Canada's!), 2001.

Building Canadarm2
on the ISS, 2001.

Playing my guitar in the
Cupola of the ISS, 2013.

Admiring the darkest dark from a window
in Space Shuttle *Atlantis,* 1995.

With Albert on Stag Island, 2015.